I0473335

This notebook belongs to:

Published by: Character Designs

Takeaway notes:

Year of use:

www.ingramcontent.com/pod-product-compliance
Lightning Source LLC
Chambersburg PA
CBHW081003170526
45158CB00010B/2888
9781072994893